Why can't I...

jump up to the moon?

and other questions
about energy

Sally Hewitt

Thameside Press

US publication copyright © Thameside Press.
International copyright reserved in all countries.
No part of this book may be reproduced in any form
without written permission from the publisher.

Distributed in the United States by
Smart Apple Media
1980 Lookout Drive
North Mankato, MN 56003

Text by Sally Hewitt 2002

ISBN 1-930643-67-5

Library of Congress Control Number 2002 141314

Series editor: Jean Coppendale
Designers: Jacqueline Palmer and Fanny Level
Picture researcher: Terry Forshaw
Consultant: Helen Walters

Printed in Hong Kong

10 9 8 7 6 5 4 3 2 1

Picture acknowledgements:
(T) = Top, (B) = Bottom, (L) = Left, (R) = Right,
(B/G) = Background, (C) = Center

Front Cover (B/G) & 16-17 © Roger Ressmeyer/Corbis; 5
(CR) & 26 (B/G) © W.Cody/Corbis; 6 (B/G) © Digital
Vision; 7 (TL) © Digital Vision, (CL) © Chrysalis Images,
(CR) © Stuart Westmorland/Corbis; 10 (B/G) ©
Galaxy/Robin Scagell; 11 (B/G) © Digital Vision, inset ©
Ecoscene/Corbis; 12 inset © Richard Hamilton
Smith/Corbis; 13 (B/G) © Ecoscene/PT; 17 (L) NASA, (R) ©
NASA/ Galaxy; 18 (B/G) © Roger Ressmeyer/Corbis; 20
(B/G) © Ecoscene/Mike Maidment; 21 inset (B/G) ©Vango
Tents; 22 inset © Martyn F.Chillmaid/Science Photo Library;
23 (B/G) © Jonathan Blair/Corbis; 24 (TR) © Joseph Sohm,
Chromo Sohm Inc/Corbis; 25 (B/G) © Ecoscene/
Nick Hawkes.

All other photography Ray Moller.

Contents

Introduction

Our world is a busy place where people and machines are hard at work.

What is happening around you now? Are you busy? Is the television on, and can you hear traffic passing by?

All of this can happen because of **energy**.

Food gives you the energy you need to grow and to be busy.

Electricity gives the television energy it needs to work.

A car burns **gasoline** for the energy to go.

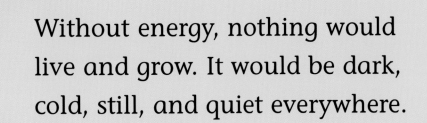

Without energy, nothing would live and grow. It would be dark, cold, still, and quiet everywhere.

But what is energy?

This book will show you how energy has the power to make things happen, and that energy on earth starts with the **sun**.

Why can't I live without the sun?

Because all the energy on earth comes from the sun.

You need energy for everything you do.

Without energy, nothing can live or grow and no work can be done.

The sun is a gigantic ball of burning gas. It sends out a huge amount of energy which gives us **heat** and **light** on earth.

Sunlight gives plants energy to grow.

Animals eat plants to give them energy.

Fruit, vegetables, and food from animals, such as meat and milk, give us the energy we need everyday.

Why does my plant need sunlight?

Because it makes its own food from the sun's rays.

Your plant doesn't look like it is working hard, but it's busy making food in its green leaves.

It uses energy from sunlight to turn air, water, and goodness from the soil into food.

Why can't I live without food?

Because food is the **fuel** that gives you energy to **work**.

1 When you feel hungry, your body is telling you that you are running out of fuel and it's time to eat.

2

3 With plenty of food inside you, you'll be ready for action.

Because the sun gives out heat and we can't see the sun at night.

The earth turns round and round in space.

When the part of the earth you are on turns away from the sun, night falls and it gets colder and dark.

10

Solar panels trap heat
energy from the sun.

This heat can warm water
even when the sun
is not shining.

Why can't I fly my kite without the wind?

Because your kite needs the wind's energy to fly.

A kite has no energy of its own.

It won't be able to fly without the wind to push it along.

Why can't I surf without waves?

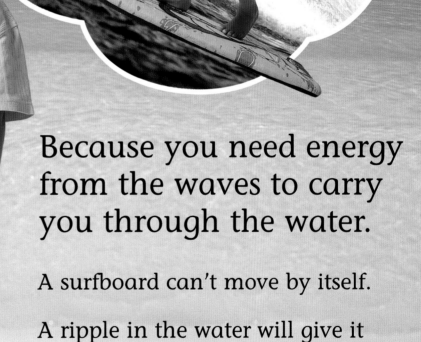

Because you need energy from the waves to carry you through the water.

A surfboard can't move by itself.

A ripple in the water will give it a small push, but the energy from a big wave will give you an exciting ride.

13

Why won't my car go without gasoline?

Because gasoline is the fuel that gives a car energy to go.

Without gas to burn, the **engine** won't have energy to turn the wheels and drive your car along.

Why can't I
jump up to the moon?

Because you don't have enough energy in your legs.

You would need a powerful rocket engine to carry you all the way to the moon.

Rocket engines are the most powerful engines ever made.

A rocket burns a huge amount of fuel to give it energy to blast away from earth and out into space.

Why can't I catch lightning?

Because the energy in lightning makes it very hot and dangerous.

Lightning is very powerful, natural electricity.

It is made when drops of water and bits of ice bump against each other inside storm clouds.

Why can't I see electricity?

Because electricity is a kind of invisible energy.

The energy from burning **coal**, gas, or oil is used to make electricity in power plants.

Then electricity flows along thick wires, called cables, from power plants into our homes.

We use electricity to make things work.

Why can't I watch television without plugging it in?

Because a television needs energy from electricity to work.

All kinds of things you use won't go without electricity.

Some of them need to be plugged in and switched on, and others are small enough to use the electricity made inside a **battery**.

Why can't I leave my flashlight on all night?

Because the batteries will go flat and your flashlight won't work.

Batteries power things you carry around, like a flashlight or a cell phone.

Chemicals inside them change to make electricity. When all the chemicals change, you need a new battery.

Why don't fireworks last forever?

Because they run out of **gunpowder**.

When the gunpowder inside fireworks is lit, it explodes in a burst of brightly colored light.

When all the gunpowder has burned, the firework fizzles out.

Why can't I play with fire?

Because the energy in fire makes it hot and it will burn you.

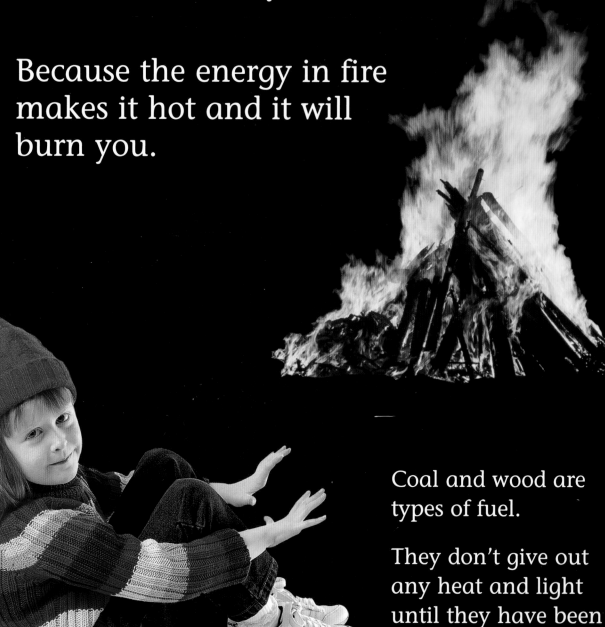

Coal and wood are types of fuel.

They don't give out any heat and light until they have been **set alight**.

Why is fire so smelly and smoky?

Because flames send smoke and soot into the air.

Smoke from burning fires makes the air dirty.

Some types of fuel make less smoke. If we burn these, we can help to keep the air clean.

Why is it important to save energy?

Because energy comes from burning fuel, and some kinds of fuel are running out.

We burn coal, gas, and oil for energy.

These fuels took millions of years to form and when they run out, they can't be replaced.

There are many ways that you can help to save energy.

Walk or cycle when you can, instead of going in the car.

Wear warm clothes instead of turning up the heating.

Don't leave the hot faucet running.

Turn off the light when you go out of a room.

Energy words

battery Batteries are little packs of energy. They are full of chemicals which change to make electricity. Small batteries are used to power things such as flashlights and radios. A big car battery is used to start a car engine.

coal Coal comes from plants that died millions of years ago. It is dug up from deep below the earth. When it is burned it gives out energy as heat and light.

electricity Electricity is a kind of energy used to power all sorts of things, from lamps to washing machines. It is made in power plants and flows along cables into our homes, schools, and places where we work.

energy Energy gives animals and machines the power to work. Heat, light, movement, and sound are some of the different sorts of energy that you can see, feel, and hear.

engine Machines such as a car or a washing machine need an engine to work them. A car engine burns gasoline to work and a washing machine engine uses electricity.

fuel Coal, oil, gas, and wood are all types of fuel. When fuel is burned, it gives out energy that can be used for heating and lighting our homes and working machines.

gasoline Gas is a type of fuel made from oil. Cars burn gasoline to give them the energy to go.

gunpowder Gunpowder is a black powder that explodes when it is set alight. Fireworks are packed with gunpowder that explodes with colorful flashes and loud bangs.

heat Heat is a kind of energy. You use it at home to keep warm and to cook your food. When things get very hot, they burn.

light Light is a kind of energy. The sun lights up the earth during the day. We use electric lights, lamps, and flashlights to light up the dark at night.

set alight When something is set alight, it catches fire and burns. Coal, wood, and candles must be set alight before they will give out heat and light energy.

solar panels Solar panels, which are built into the roofs of some houses, store heat from the sun. This heat then warms-up water running along pipes.

sun The sun is a ball of burning gas in space that gives out heat and light energy. The earth gets all its energy from the sun.

work Every time something moves, lights up, gives out heat, or makes a sound, it works. Nothing can work without energy.

Activities

Here is a group of things that need energy to work. Match each one to the fuel it uses to give it energy. Some things may work on more than one kind of fuel.

- You
- Television
- Flashlight
- Car
- Radiator
- Stove
- Fire
- Radio
- Computer
- Truck
- Light
- Cat

Electricity
Food
Battery
Oil
Coal
Gasoline
Gas

These words describe different types of energy.
Sort them into groups with these headings:

- Heat energy
- Light energy
- Sound energy
- Movement energy

hot bright quiet fast cold dark loud slow freezing shiny noisy falling boiling dull booming flying

Can you think of more words to go into each group?

Notes for parents and teachers

Children know they can't jump to the moon, but they may not know the reason why. Spend some time together thinking about the questions in this book and the possibilities they raise before reading the simple, factual answers. You may like to try out these activities with your child. They will reinforce what you have learned about energy, and give you plenty to discuss.

Sun, wind, and water

You can use energy from the sun, wind, and running water to generate heat and help make things move.

• Leave a brick outside in warm sunshine for as long as you can. Take the brick inside and feel how warm it has become. It has stored up heat energy from the sun.

• Fly a kite on a windy day. Feel the kite tugging the string as the wind pushes it up into the air.

• Push a pencil through an empty spool of thread and hold it under a running faucet. Watch the water spin the spool.

Batteries

Take the battery out of a flashlight and see how each end is different. Does the flashlight work whatever way you put it back? Can you work out how the switch turns the light on and off?

Use some energy

You use energy reading a book, walking, and running. Try doing each of these activities and see how much energy you use. Which can you do for the longest amount of time without getting tired? How can you tell which uses the most energy?

31

Index